SPELLS
&
CHARMS

A MOVIE SCRAPBOOK

WIZARDING
WORLD

BLOOMSBURY
CHILDREN'S BOOKS
LONDON OXFORD NEW YORK NEW DELHI SYDNEY

An Insight Editions Book

CONTENTS

INTRODUCTION

When first-year student Hermione Granger meets fellow classmates Harry Potter and Ron Weasley during their train trip to Hogwarts School of Witchcraft and Wizardry, she notices that Ron has his wand poised over his rat, Scabbers. 'Oh,' she says, 'are you doing magic? Let's see then.' Unfortunately, the spell Ron's brother Fred gave him to turn the rat yellow proves to be a dud. 'Are you sure that's a real spell?' she scolds. 'Well, it's not very good, is it. Of course, I've only tried a few simple ones myself, but they've all worked for me.' Then the young witch casts *Oculus Reparo* to fix Harry's broken glasses, demonstrating early on just how good she is at spell work.

The Muggle world defines spells and charms as 'a spoken word or set of words *believed* to have magical power'. Muggles who have seen the Harry Potter films set in J.K. Rowling's Wizarding World know that there is no doubt: the magical results of the spells cast on-screen are entirely believable.

For *Harry Potter and the Order of the Phoenix*, director David Yates desired a clearly defined language of wand movements. 'When magic's been done in films before, it's always been sort of 'just do it and say the words'', says Daniel Radcliffe, who plays the title character, 'and we've done that to a certain extent in these films. But David was keen to actually make a distinction between how very advanced wizards do the spells and how young wizards, rookie wizards, do them.' Daniel felt that the wand choreography developed by dancer and choreographer Paul Harris did just that. 'Obviously, it's the intention behind the spell and how much you actually want to perform the spell,' Daniel says, 'but it is also the movement, which was fun to do, but I found quite challenging. I've ended up, I think, getting it. I hope!'

There are only a few requirements for performing a spell or charm. Proper pronunciation of the charm's incantation is a must, lest you risk your feather exploding when casting *Wingardium Leviosa*. The wizard also must accompany the spell with the right physical movements and have a wand that is in good working order, or the spell may backfire upon the caster. And finally, spell work should be done with firm intention. You must really be committed to bringing about the effects of the spell.

So, wands at the ready! It's time to study spells, cast charms and make some magic.

SPELLS
&
CHARMS

WINGARDIUM LEVIOSA

The first lesson Charms professor Filius Flitwick gives first-year students is *Wingardium Leviosa*, a Levitation Charm with which they attempt to make an object – in this case a feather – rise up. He reminds them to follow a precise wand movement: 'Swish and flick.'

SPELL ESSENTIALS

INTENTION:
Charm to levitate objects

KNOWN USERS:
Hermione Granger, Ron Weasley, Harry Potter

APPEARANCES:
Harry Potter and the Philosopher's Stone, Harry Potter and the Chamber of Secrets

LESSON LEARNED

Ron Weasley is annoyed by Hermione Granger's assistance during Charms class, but proves he listened to her when a troll invades Hogwarts castle on Halloween and traps Hermione in a girls' bathroom. Ron casts the spell so that the troll's heavy club floats up and then drops down on its head, knocking it out. T̶h̶e̶ ̶t̶r̶o̶l̶l̶ was mostly a digital creature, but its lower half was crea̶t̶e̶d̶ ̶f̶o̶r̶ ̶E̶mma Watson to scoot around as she tries to hide unde̶r̶ ̶o̶n̶e̶ ̶o̶f̶ ̶t̶h̶e̶ exploding sinks.

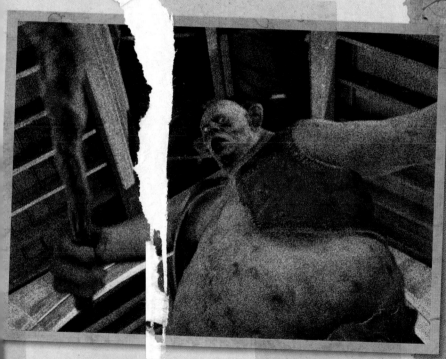

BREAKING EVEN

The special effects team built huge clubs on mechanical rigs that would swing around to smash the toilets and doors. The destruction was designed to occur at what they estimated to be 'troll speed', so when the troll was created on the computer, its movements interacted perfectly with the practical clubs.

Prior to her first year at Hogwarts, Hermione had already tried out a few spells successfully, like *Oculus Reparo*, which she uses to fix Harry's glasses. In her first year, she shows just how skilled she is with these spells:

ALOHOMORA:
Charm to open locked doors

LACARNUM INFLAMARI:
Charm to start a fire

LUMOS SOLEM:
Charm that sends a powerful ray of light as bright as the sun out of caster's wand

PETRIFICUS TOTALUS:
Spell that paralyses the target temporarily

PESKIPIKSI PESTERNOMI

The *Peskipiksi Pesternomi* charm used by Defence Against the Dark Arts professor Gilderoy Lockhart is of questionable origin and questionable value. In his first lesson, Lockhart releases a cage of Cornish pixies into his classroom, who proceed to make a mess and buzz around the students. His charm does nothing to round them up.

SPELL ESSENTIALS

INTENTION:
Charm to immobilise pixies

KNOWN USERS:
Gilderoy Lockhart (unsuccessful)

APPEARANCES:
Harry Potter and the Chamber of Secrets

CHAOS AND CLUTTER

The ill-behaved Cornish pixies throw books off shelves and pull students' hair. While the Cornish pixies themselves were computer-generated, these actions were practical effects, done by using thin wires. Matthew Lewis, who plays Neville Longbottom, wore clips on his ears to create the effect of two pixies pulling him up to hang him from the classroom chandelier. Matthew says that this scene included his favourite line in all the films: 'Why is it always me?'

IMMOBULUS

As Lockhart escapes to his office, he asks Harry, Ron and Hermione to get the destructive creatures back into their cage. Quick-thinking Hermione is the first out with her wand, casting *Immobulus*, a charm that freezes its targets in place. The pixies are brought to a halt and hover in place, unable to move.

EXTRA CREDIT

Gilderoy Lockhart's documented triumphs are due to his talent with *Obliviate*, a Memory Charm; he publishes other wizards' achievements as his own after erasing their memories. But when he uses Ron's damaged wand to cast *Obliviate* on his student, the charm backfires and the teacher loses his own memory.

ARANIA EXUMAI

Harry and Ron visit the Forbidden Forest to speak with Aragog, an Acromantula who might be able to help them identify the Heir of Slytherin. When they try to leave, Aragog's colony of offspring descends upon them, hoping for a tasty treat. Harry casts *Arania Exumai*, which blasts the spiders away and prevents them from attacking Harry and Ron.

SPELL ESSENTIALS

INTENTION:
Spell to repel spiders from caster

KNOWN USERS:
Harry Potter, Tom Riddle

APPEARANCES:
Harry Potter and the Chamber of Secrets

Founding Father

The two-storey high Aragog was not a digital effect like his children but built and performed practically. 'I don't like spiders in real life,' says Rupert Grint (who portrayed Ron Weasley). 'I even get really scared of rubber ones.' So, what was his first meeting with Aragog like? 'Horrible! When I saw Aragog for the first time, I wasn't acting; I was genuinely scared.'

Harry learns *Arania Exumai* while viewing a memory from Tom Riddle's diary. When Tom releases the young Aragog from a container, he casts this spell in an attempt to destroy the spider.

YOURS DROOLY

Hagrid's dog, Fang, accompanies Ron and Harry into the Forbidden Forest but proves to be a coward when he jumps into the Ford Anglia, which helps them escape. An animatronic version of Fang – which could not only move, but drool – sat in the car.

◇ EXTRA CREDIT ◇

Fifty years prior, the Chamber of Secrets was opened and a female student was killed. To avoid any suspicion and keep Hogwarts from being closed, Tom Riddle accuses Hagrid of harbouring the monster that killed the girl. He blasts open a locked container with *Cistem Aperio*, a charm used exclusively to open boxes, trunks or crates. Aragog, the innocent Acromantula inside, scurries away.

DUELLING CLUB SPELLS

Professor Lockhart starts a Duelling Club as an additional tool to train the students in defensive magic. He is 'assisted' by Professor Severus Snape.

EXPELLIARMUS

The *Expelliarmus* spell is used to remove an object from an opponent's hand. In their demonstration duel, Severus Snape uses this to whip Lockhart's wand from his hand.

EVERTE STATUM

When Draco Malfoy is pitted against Harry Potter in a duel, he casts *Everte Statum*, a spell that causes one's duelling opponent to be hurled backwards.

* * ✷ * *

ROLLING OVER

Tom Felton (Draco Malfoy) wore his own wire rig in order to perform his stunt for *Rictusempra*, which has more of a rolling movement. 'It was a lot of fun,' Tom remembers. 'That was pretty exciting, doing our own stunts at thirteen or fourteen.'

Harry Potter strikes back at Draco with a comparable spell, the *Rictusempra* charm, which also sends one's opponent backwards.

UP AND OVER

Daniel Radcliffe (Harry Potter) wore a wire rig that flipped him up and over when hit by *Everte Statum*. 'Basically, there was a wire that came down my front,' says Daniel, 'and then carefully around to my back to the pick point of a harness, so that when they pulled the wire, I spun out of it and around.'

SERPENSORTIA

Draco retaliates with the *Serpensortia* spell, which conjures a serpent out of the caster's wand – in this case, a cobra. Harry unknowingly speaks Parseltongue to keep the snake from attacking anyone.

* * *

ALARTE ASCENDARE

Lockhart tries to remove the snake with *Alarte Ascendare*, a spell used to toss an object into the air. It lifts the snake up but then just drops it down in the same place.

* * *

VIPERA EVANESCA

Snape ends the snake's existence by using *Vipera Evanesca*, a counterspell to *Serpensortia*, which makes the snake vanish.

RIDDIKULUS

Boggarts are shape-shifting creatures that take the form of what we fear the most. As Defence Against the Dark Arts professor Remus Lupin explains to his students for his class on Boggarts: 'You need to force it to assume a shape you find truly amusing.' Then the Boggart can be easily defeated by laughter. The incantation that accomplishes this intention is the *Riddikulus* spell.

SPELL ESSENTIALS

INTENTION:
Charm to defeat a Boggart

KNOWN USERS:
Remus Lupin, Neville Longbottom,
Ron Weasley, Parvati Patil

APPEARANCES:
Harry Potter and the Prisoner of Azkaban

IN THE IN-BETWEEN

The first and final shapes for each student's Boggart were easy to create for the films: Ron dresses an Acromantula in eight roller skates; Parvati Patil turns a cobra into a jack-in-the-box. A challenge for the visual effects designers was what a Boggart looked like in between its transformations. Director Alfonso Cuarón didn't want it to be solid, nor did he want it to be transparent. The designers took the fearsome and funny versions of the Boggart and mashed them up in a tornado-type whirlwind.

No Laughing Matter

Neville Longbottom's worst fear is, not surprisingly, Professor Snape. At Lupin's suggestion, Neville succeeds in dressing the Boggart Snape in his grandmother's clothes, including her bird-topped hat. When asked what his character would have thought about the transformation, actor Alan Rickman said, 'Snape isn't one who enjoys jokes – I strongly fear that his sense of humour is extremely limited.'

SPELLS TAUGHT TO DUMBLEDORE'S ARMY

Dolores Umbridge, the Defence Against the Dark Arts professor in Harry Potter's fifth year at Hogwarts, refuses to teach her students defensive magic. With the threat of Voldemort's return looming over them, Hermione recruits Harry to privately teach any interested students. Meeting in the Room of Requirement, this underground resistance movement calls themselves 'Dumbledore's Army'.

EXPELLIARMUS

The Disarming Charm is essential to any wand battle – it literally forces an opponent's wand out of his or her hand.

SPELL ESSENTIALS

INTENTION:
Charm to remove something from opponent's hand

KNOWN USERS:
Severus Snape, Remus Lupin, James Potter, Harry Potter, Cedric Diggory, Neville Longbottom, Luna Lovegood, Cho Chang, Draco Malfoy, Hermione Granger, Ron Weasley

APPEARANCES:
Harry Potter and the Chamber of Secrets, Harry Potter and the Prisoner of Azkaban, Harry Potter and the Goblet of Fire, Harry Potter and the Order of the Phoenix, Harry Potter and the Half-Blood Prince, Harry Potter and the Deathly Hallows – Parts 1 and 2

STUPEFY

The Stunning Spell knocks out the caster's opponent, causing them to be become semi- or totally unconscious. As Harry tells the members of Dumbledore's Army, 'It's sort of a wizard's bread-and-butter.'

SPELL ESSENTIALS

INTENTION:
Spell to knock out caster's opponent

KNOWN USERS:
Nigel Wolpert, Hermione Granger, Ron Weasley, Neville Longbottom, Luna Lovegood, Ginny Weasley, Harry Potter

APPEARANCES:
Harry Potter and the Goblet of Fire, Harry Potter and the Order of the Phoenix, Harry Potter and the Half-Blood Prince, Harry Potter and the Deathly Hallows – Parts 1 and *2*

ALL TIED UP

In training, Hermione hits Ron with *Stupefy*. 'Ron goes in all cocky, thinking he can beat a girl,' says Rupert Grint. 'I fly back when Hermione disarms me and [get] very embarrassed by it.' Rupert was wired up to do a stunt called a *pullback*. 'We don't get to do [stunts] that often, but when [we] do, they're really cool.'

REDUCTO

The Reductor Curse reduces solid targets to pieces. Ginny Weasley uses it to destroy the practice opponent in the Room of Requirement and then again in the Hall of Prophecy, causing the shelves in the room to come crashing down.

SPELL ESSENTIALS

INTENTION:
Curse to reduce solid targets to small pieces

KNOWN USERS:
Harry Potter, Ginny Weasley, Hermione Granger

APPEARANCES:
Harry Potter and the Goblet of Fire, Harry Potter and the Order of the Phoenix, Harry Potter and the Deathly Hallows – Parts 1 and *2*

EXPECTO PATRONUM

The most advanced spell or charm Harry Potter teaches Dumbledore's Army is the Patronus Charm, which is the best defence against Dementors. There are two types of Patronuses: corporeal, which takes the shape of an animal with a unique meaning to its caster, or an unremarkable noncorporeal shape. Harry's corporeal Patronus is a stag, just like his father's.

SPELL ESSENTIALS

INTENTION:
Charm to create a Patronus

KNOWN USERS:
Remus Lupin, Harry Potter, Hermione Granger, Ron Weasley, Luna Lovegood, Ginny Weasley, Kingsley Shacklebolt, Aberforth Dumbledore, Severus Snape

APPEARANCES:
Harry Potter and the Prisoner of Azkaban, Harry Potter and the Order of the Phoenix, Harry Potter and the Deathly Hallows – Parts 1 and *2*

GLOWING TERMS

Harry learns the Patronus Charm in his third year when Dementors roam the Hogwarts grounds. Professor Remus Lupin teaches him to think of the happiest memory he can when casting the charm, and eventually a shield form emerges from his wand against a Boggart who has transformed into a Dementor. Different digital versions of the Patronus effect were tested before the final design was reached, with names like 'blow torch', 'liquid metal', and 'silly string'.

LET IT SHINE

Harry is rewarded as a teacher when many of his students are able to conjure a Patronus. Ginny casts a horse with a fluttering mane, Hermione conjures a playful otter, and Ron conjures an equally playful Jack Russell terrier that knocks Neville over. The digital programs that crafted these ephemeral creatures were able to individualise them with shimmering ripples and pulsating patterns. Trailing ribbons of light that dissolved as the Patronuses moved gave them a sense of direction and energy.

The visual designers didn't know Ron's Patronus was a dog when they started their designs, and so they first envisioned it as a fox. Among other possible Patronuses for Ron were a chimpanzee and a Thestral.

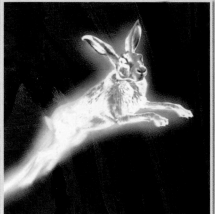

◈ EXTRA CREDIT ◈

Nigel uses the *Diminuendo* charm to shrink the Dumbledore's Army practice dummy.

✳ ✳ ✴ ✳ ✳

◈ EXTRA CREDIT ◈

Levicorpus is a jinx to raise a human target into the air, usually by their ankle. Luna casts *Levicorpus* at a Death Eater while escaping the Hall of Prophecy.

TRIWIZARD STRATEGIES

In *Harry Potter and the Goblet of Fire*, Hogwarts hosts the Triwizard Tournament, an international competition between wizarding schools. Beauxbatons Academy of Magic and Durmstrang Institute join Hogwarts in sending their champions to compete in the contest; they must use spells and charms in order to succeed at three tasks that will lead one of them to win the Triwizard Cup.

BUBBLE-HEAD CHARM

The second task required the champions to be underwater for up to an hour. After rescuing Cho Chang, Hufflepuff champion Cedric Diggory was awarded first place for – as Albus Dumbledore announces – his 'innate command of the Bubble-Head Charm'. Artwork by Adam Brockbank visualised how the charm would work.

ACCIO

For his battle against a dragon in the first task of the Triwizard Tournament, Harry Potter is encouraged by Alastor Moody to use his best skills. Armed with only his wand, Harry summons his broom using *Accio Firebolt*.

SPELL ESSENTIALS
(Incantation Unknown)

INTENTION:
Charm that creates a bubble of air around caster's head

KNOWN USERS:
Cedric Diggory

APPEARANCES:
Harry Potter and the Goblet of Fire

SPELL ESSENTIALS

INTENTION:
Charm to summon an object

KNOWN USERS:
Molly Weasley, Hermione Granger, Harry Potter, Barty Crouch Jr (disguised as Alastor 'Mad-Eye' Moody), Ron Weasley, Fred and George Weasley, Lord Voldemort

APPEARANCES:
Harry Potter and the Goblet of Fire, Harry Potter and the Deathly Hallows – Parts 1 and 2

IN THE SWIM

Filming the underwater scenes took place in a 60 x 20 x 20-foot tank and required the actors to learn to scuba dive. Robert Pattinson (who portrayed Cedric Diggory) hadn't had much swimming experience, so his lessons began in a very small pool, which was 'more or less a bathtub,' he remembers. After three weeks, he graduated to a 'proper pool,' before working in the large tank. 'But there were so many divers and safety people around that I never felt the slightest bit scared.'

ASCENDIO

During the second task, Harry is surrounded by a swarm of impish Grindylows, who try to drag him down into the Black Lake. Harry uses *Ascendio* to disentangle himself and shoot out of the water.

SPELL ESSENTIALS

INTENTION:
Spell to lift caster upwards

KNOWN USERS:
Harry Potter

APPEARANCES:
Harry Potter and the Goblet of Fire

PERICULUM

In order to save Fleur Delacour from being overcome and strangled by the maze's branches in the third task, Harry Potter casts the *Periculum* charm to signal for help in rescuing the Beauxbatons champion.

SPELL ESSENTIALS

INTENTION:
Charm that sends red sparks upwards out of the caster's wand

KNOWN USERS:
Harry Potter

APPEARANCE:
Harry Potter and the Goblet of Fire

IMPROPER SPELLS

Magic can backfire when the spell is not done correctly.

'Sunshine, daisies, butter mellow, Turn this stupid fat rat yellow.'

RATS!

During his first trip to Hogwarts on the Hogwarts Express, Ron Weasley tries a bit of magic given to him by his brother Fred to change his rat, Scabbers, to a different colour, but the end result is only a flash of light and a very confused rat.

LIVE WIRE

An animatronic Scabbers plays the part when the rat is first digging around in a box of Bertie Bott's Every Flavour Beans on Ron's lap. Once the spell is cast, Scabbers backs out of the box. For this, a real rat named Dex had a box attached to a wire gently placed over his head by a trainer. Once the cue was given, the trainer pulled the wire and the box came off – making it appear as if Scabbers had backed out.

AVOID CASTING ANY SPELL WITH A DAMAGED WAND!

EAT SLUGS!

Ron's wand is broken in *Harry Potter and the Chamber of Secrets* when he and Harry land in the Whomping Willow. He tries to fix it with Spellotape, but it's a no go. When he yells 'Eat slugs!' and tries to cast a vengeful slug-vomiting spell at Draco Malfoy, the spell rebounds and it's Ron who ends up spitting out the slimy creatures. Luckily, the plastic slug props were flavoured lemon, orange, chocolate, and peppermint.

PROTECTIVE ENCHANTMENTS

In *Harry Potter and the Deathly Hallows – Part 1*, Harry, Ron and Hermione are on the run from Death Eaters and Ministry of Magic mercenaries called 'Snatchers'. After they Apparate to the Forest of Dean to escape, Hermione fortifies the area with protective enchantments.

◇ PROTEGO TOTALUM ◇

The *Protego* charm, a variation of a Shield Charm, creates a barrier between the caster and his or her opponent. Spells and charms can bounce off the barrier, sometimes back on to their caster. Adding *Totalum* gives the charm maximum strength.

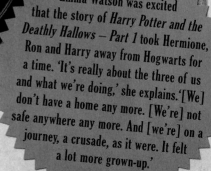

Emma Watson was excited that the story of *Harry Potter and the Deathly Hallows – Part 1* took Hermione, Ron and Harry away from Hogwarts for a time. 'It's really about the three of us and what we're doing,' she explains. '[We] don't have a home any more. [We're] not safe anywhere any more. And [we're] on a journey, a crusade, as it were. It felt a lot more grown-up.'

SALVIO HEXIA

The *Salvio Hexia* charm is another form of protective shield, this time specific to hexes.

* * * * *

MUFFLIATO

The *Muffliato* charm deadens the sound around the caster so they cannot be heard.

* * * * *

REPELLO MUGGLETUM

The Muggle-Repelling Charm is just that – a charm to repel Muggles from a shielded location. This charm also may have been used to keep Muggles from the Leaky Cauldron in London and the Quidditch World Cup matches.

DISILLUSIONMENT CHARM

Unfortunately, Snatchers discover Hermione, Ron and Harry after they Apparate to a new location and before they can cast protective spells. In order to keep Harry safe before they're captured, Hermione casts the Stinging Jinx at him and his face swells up, concealing his appearance. The designers referenced mumps and other disfiguring diseases for the Stinging Jinx's effect.

ON THE RUN

Harry, Ron and Hermione run from the Snatchers, who pursue them through a hilly, leaf-covered forest. The shoot took place over the course of a week and utilised different filming techniques, including a camera that zipped along a line strung between the trees. 'And we had a camera mounted on a motorbike that chased us,' says Rupert Grint. 'That really makes you run even faster.'

FACE ON

Daniel Radcliffe's face was covered with prosthetics for the effect; only one eye was left exposed. But the fake pieces still needed to look like Daniel, so make-up artists punched eyebrows and beard stubble into the prosthetics – one hair at a time.

DOUBLING CHARM

The Gemino Curse is used to create a double of an object, although the duplication will deteriorate over time. This charm can also be used to force an object to make endless multiples of itself when it is touched.

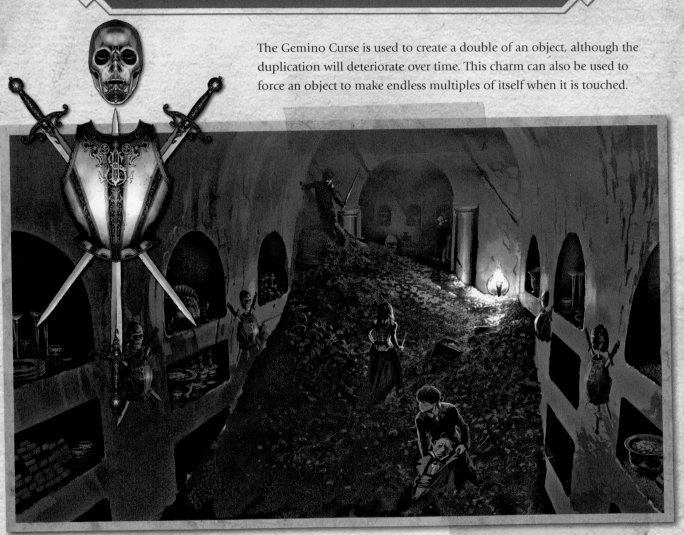

TWO FOR ONE

When Hermione, Harry and Ron sneak into the Lestrange vault at Gringotts Wizarding Bank to locate the Hufflepuff Cup, Hermione and Ron accidentally touch treasure pieces, which then begin duplicating. As these and other items bounce and bump into each other, the room quickly fills up with copies.

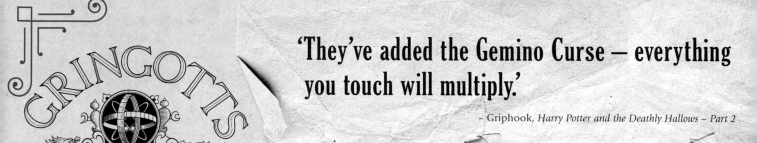

GRINGOTTS

'They've added the Gemino Curse — everything you touch will multiply.'

– Griphook, *Harry Potter and the Deathly Hallows – Part 2*

SPELL ESSENTIALS

INTENTION:
Curse to cause duplication
of any object

KNOWN USERS:
The Lestrange family

APPEARANCES:
*Harry Potter and the Deathly
Hallows – Part 2*

FILLED TO THE BRIM

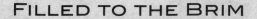

Though their moment of duplication was achieved digitally, the multiplying treasures that filled the vault were created practically. The prop department used an injection-moulding machine, which ran on a twenty-four-hour schedule in order to fill over 700 cubic feet of space with soft plastic copies of six different items. 'It's like one of those children's ball pits,' props art director Hattie Storey explains. 'But here you wade through treasure and gold.'

IMPERIO

There are three sinister spells that are so unforgivable they are actually called the 'Unforgivable Curses', and their use is punishable by imprisonment in Azkaban. In Harry Potter's fourth year, ex-Auror Alastor 'Mad-Eye' Moody takes the position of Defence Against the Dark Arts teacher. His students are stunned by his first lesson, which is on the Unforgivable Curses. It's later discovered that Death Eater Barty Crouch Jr has kidnapped Moody and used Polyjuice Potion to impersonate him at the school.

SPELL ESSENTIALS

INTENTION:
Causes a target to be under the caster's control

KNOWN USERS:
Barty Crouch Jr (disguised as Alastor Moody), Voldemort (non-verbal), Harry Potter

APPEARANCES:
Harry Potter and the Goblet of Fire, Harry Potter and the Deathly Hallows – Part 2

Undue Influence

The Imperius Curse causes the caster's victim to be under their control. Those who have been Imperiused may be difficult to spot, as victims often appear calm and even happily obedient. The fake Moody shows the darker side of this curse when he casts it on an arachnid during class. He flies the spider around the classroom, dropping it on students' heads and faces (poor Ron!) and then threatens to have it fly out the window or drown it.

Pre-Curled Hair and Makeup

To enter the Lestrange vault at Gringotts in *Harry Potter and the Deathly Hallows – Part 2*, Harry uses *Imperio* on the goblin bank teller Bogrod. The Gringotts goblins' faces (sixty of them!) featured prosthetics made from a silicone that comes up to body temperature when applied. Each goblin had their hairlines and eyebrows created by inserting one pre-curled hair at a time.

Hold Your Tongue

Harry first asks Griphook the goblin, played by Warwick Davis, to help him get into the Gringotts vaults. It took Warwick four hours each day to transform into Griphook. He wore black contact lenses and dentures with very sharp teeth. 'I had to be very careful when I talked during a scene,' says Warwick. 'If I wasn't, I'd bite my tongue, which happened a bit too often for me.'

EXTRA CREDIT

When the fake Professor Moody begins his lesson on Unforgivable Curses, he uses an Engorgement Charm on a spider to make it big enough for the entire class to see. In *Harry Potter and the Deathly Hallows – Part 1*, Harry casts *Engorgio* to increase a flame contained in a bottle, which shoots up like a volcanic eruption.

* * *

EXTRA CREDIT

Reducio is the counterspell to *Engorgio* and will shrink an object back to its original size.

CRUCIO

The Cruciatus Curse inflicts unbearable pain upon its victims, brutalising them into insanity in extreme cases. It also is known as the Torture Curse. When Neville Longbottom was an infant, the Death Eater Bellatrix Lestrange used the Cruciatus Curse on his parents, who were both members of the Order of the Phoenix. Lestrange did not get any information as a result, but the Curse left both of her victims mentally injured.

SPIDER SYMPATHY

The fake Professor Moody calls Neville to the front of the class to watch the effects of *Crucio* on the large spider. 'That was pretty freaky,' says Matthew Lewis (who plays Neville). He didn't mind the fountain of maggots on the desk but wasn't thrilled by the amblypygid, or tailless scorpion spider. Like actor Rupert Grint (who plays Ron), Matthew has arachnophobia. 'So that was not nice,' he remembers.

An Unforgivable Trifecta

After Voldemort is brought back to life in the Little Hangleton graveyard in *Harry Potter and the Goblet of Fire*, he casts the Cruciatus Curse on Harry. In fact, the Dark Lord uses all three Unforgivable Curses on Harry during their encounter, as it can be assumed that Voldemort uses the Imperius Curse to force Harry to bow before their wand duel and he later tries to cast the Killing Curse, *Avada Kedavra*, in Harry's direction.

Storyboards show Harry attempting to cast the Cruciatus Curse at Bellatrix but not achieving it. When Harry is distracted by Voldemort's appearance, Bellatrix escapes through one of the thirty-foot-high fireplaces at the Ministry of Magic.

Intents and Purposes

In *Harry Potter and the Order of the Phoenix*, Harry chases Bellatrix Lestrange after she kills his godfather, Sirius Black, and tries to cast the Cruciatus Curse at her. But the caster of this curse needs a strong intention to cause someone physical pain, and Harry does not succeed.

SPELL ESSENTIALS

INTENTION:
Tortures the target of the caster with pain

KNOWN USERS:
Barty Crouch Jr (disguised as Alastor Moody), Voldemort, Bellatrix Lestrange, Harry Potter (unsuccessful)

APPEARANCES:
Harry Potter and the Goblet of Fire, Harry Potter and the Order of the Phoenix

There is only one known survivor of the third Unforgivable Curse, *Avada Kedavra*, also known as the Killing Curse: Harry Potter. When Harry was an infant, the Dark Lord Voldemort unsuccessfully attempted to kill him with this curse, but he was protected from the spell by his mother's loving sacrifice (the ultimate magical protection). When Voldemort tried it again during Harry's fourth year at Hogwarts, the clash of Voldemort's and Harry's wands led to Priori Incantatem, which nullified the curse.

DRAWING NEAR

Though Voldemort was not able to kill Harry as an infant, he did leave his mark: a lightning-bolt-shaped scar on Harry's forehead. The scar was replicated on actor Daniel Radcliffe more than two thousand times throughout the eight films. Chief makeup artist Amanda Knight changed the scar subtly depending on Harry's nearness to Voldemort. 'When Voldemort was near Harry, we'd make Harry slightly paler,' she explains. 'At the same time, we'd make his scar stronger, redder, and more angry-looking.'

STAYING POWER

Voldemort unwittingly transferred some of his own powers to the infant Harry when he cursed him, such as being able to speak Parseltongue. Harry does 'die' when Voldemort casts *Avada Kedavra* a third time, but in that case, what Voldemort kills is the part of himself left in Harry.

NON-VERBAL SPELLS

PRIORI INCANTATEM

When two wands with cores from the same creature connect in battle, this can result in Priori Incantatem: the reverse spell effect. This is the case with the wands of Harry Potter and Lord Voldemort, both of which contain feathers from Albus Dumbledore's phoenix, Fawkes. In a struggle of willpower, one wand forces the other to reveal its past spells. If one of those spells is the Killing Curse, *Avada Kedavra*, a shadowy echo of the victim appears. Multiple victims will appear in the reverse order of their deaths.

SPELL ESSENTIALS

(Unintentional spell created by twin wand cores in battle)

KNOWN USERS:
Voldemort, Harry Potter

APPEARANCES:
Harry Potter and the Goblet of Fire

A BUNDLE OF ENERGY

As Harry's and Voldemort's wands collide in the Little Hangleton graveyard, the stretch of energy between them connects together in a white-hot explosion. Visual effects supervisor Tim Burke describes it as 'plasma-like energy shifts that dripped a molten lava substance'.

Lost Connections

Voldemort's and Harry's wands link again in *Harry Potter and the Deathly Hallows – Part 2*. But in the time since their previous battle, Voldemort has acquired another wand; the stolen Elder Wand. And Harry's wand was destroyed while escaping Nagini in Godric's Hollow in *Deathly Hallows – Part 1*; he's been using Draco Malfoy's wand, taken in Malfoy Manor. So the two wands cannot create Priori Incantatem.

Hot Stuff

Albus Dumbledore's and Lord Voldemort's wands collide and connect as they begin their battle in the Ministry of Magic in *Harry Potter and the Order of the Phoenix*. The visual effects designers referenced the wand-to-wand duel between Harry and Voldemort from *Goblet of Fire*. The dripping energy spatters were made even brighter, and lens flares were added to enhance the effect.

SECTUMSEMPRA

The wounds and the blood that reddens Draco's shirt and seeps into the water on the bathroom floor were completely digital effects.

Harry Potter discovers the *Sectumsempra* curse in the Half-Blood Prince's *Advanced Potion-Making* textbook. It's clearly marked 'For Enemies'. When Harry follows Draco Malfoy into a private bathroom, suspicious of his mysterious behaviour, a duel results that ends in Harry casting the curse, not knowing its consequences.

SPELL ESSENTIALS

INTENTION:
Curse that slashes victims from a distance

KNOWN USERS:
Harry Potter

APPEARANCES:
Harry Potter and the Half-Blood Prince

Real Reactions

Director David Yates wanted scenes to be as realistic as they could be with the actors on set, and so the fight in the bathroom included many practical as well as digital effects. 'The special effects guys rigged [it] for blowing bits of cubicle out, smashing sinks, and breaking mirrors,' explains Tim Burke. 'And on top of that, we enhanced the wand hits, adding various bits of debris.' Tim describes shooting the sequence as if it was a gunfight.

'They rigged the whole bathroom, literally, with explosives,' says Tom Felton. Every time Draco or Harry fired a spell, something would explode. 'That was good for us,' he adds. 'It was very exciting.'

COUNTERCURSE

VULNERA SANENTUR

As Severus Snape, the Half-Blood Prince, created the *Sectumsempra* curse, he fortunately created a countercurse: *Vulnera Sanentur*. As he touches his wand to Draco's wounds, he intones the singsong incantation, and the blood and injuries disappear.

EXPLOSIVE SPELLS

Several spells and curses can cause varying degrees of fiery or explosive results.

BOMBARDA / BOMBARDA MAXIMA

The Exploding Charm, *Bombarda*, produces a small explosion, which can be intensified by adding *Maxima* to the spell.

Hermione Granger uses *Bombarda* to quickly open the bars that imprison Sirius Black at Hogwarts in *Harry Potter and the Prisoner of Azkaban*.

SPELL ESSENTIALS

INTENTION:
Charm to blast an encumbrance open or explode a target

KNOWN USERS:
Hermione Granger, Dolores Umbridge

APPEARANCES:
Harry Potter and the Prisoner of Azkaban, Harry Potter and the Order of the Phoenix

BREAKING AND ENTERING

Suspicious of some of her students' activities, Dolores Umbridge sends her Inquisitorial Squad to find out where Harry and the other members of Dumbledore's Army are going when they disappear into the Room of Requirement. Umbridge casts *Bombarda Maxima* to blow open an entrance to the hidden room.

Wall to Wall

The special effects crew created the *Bombarda Maxima* explosion by replacing the outer wall of the Room of Requirement with cork. The mirrored interior wall was reconstructed with a reflective material that was laser cut with a predetermined break pattern. Between the two fake walls was a space filled with compressed air that allowed for a safe explosion when the radio-controlled effect was triggered.

CONFRINGO

Confringo, or the Blasting Curse, hits a target with a fiery charge of energy. Hermione uses *Confringo* in an effort to escape Nagini in *Harry Potter and the Deathly Hallows – Part 1*, and Harry uses it to try to kill the snake in *Part 2*.

✳ ✳ ✳

EXPULSO

The Expulso Curse creates an intense explosive force. Hermione uses it in *Harry Potter and the Deathly Hallows – Part 1* during a wand battle in the London café against Death Eaters, and Harry casts it in an effort to open the Slytherin Locket Horcrux.

✳ ✳ ✳

INCENDIO

Hermione also tries *Incendio*, the Fire-Making Charm, which lights objects on fire, on the Slytherin Locket Horcrux.

FIENDFYRE

Fiendfyre, which is capable of seeking out living targets despite being non-sentient, is extremely difficult to control and cannot be put out with water. Gregory Goyle produces Fiendfyre in the Room of Requirement in *Harry Potter and the Deathly Hallows – Part 2*, which was a combination of digital effects and controlled flames and flare-ups.

SPELL ESSENTIALS

(Incantation Unknown)

INTENTION:
Curse that creates a bewitched inextinguishable fire

KNOWN USERS:
Gregory Goyle

APPEARANCES:
Harry Potter and the Deathly Hallows – Part 2

Note: Fiendfyre can destroy Horcruxes.

SHAKE, RATTLE, AND ROLL

Draco Malfoy and Blaise Zabini attempt to escape the Fiendfyre atop a rickety mountain of tables and chairs. 'We rigged that so the furniture was shaky and wobbly while they were climbing,' says special effects supervisor John Richardson, 'but, of course, it was completely safe.'

UP FOR GRABS

Wired for safety, Tom Felton (Draco Malfoy) and Louis Cordice (Blaise Zabini) had to stand on a small table after they completed their climb. Then the table's legs were made to collapse, and the actors needed to quickly turn and grab the tabletop. One challenge for Felton was that he knew the table was going to collapse and was anticipating it, so it took several takes. 'We got the shot in the end,' says Tom. 'It's brilliantly shot, so it looks natural, but that was the most terrifying stunt.' Adds stunt coordinator Greg Powell, 'The look on their faces – that is genuine.'

HOGWARTS CASTLE DEFENSIVE CHARMS

As Voldemort's forces arrive at Hogwarts, Professor Flitwick, Professor Slughorn and Molly Weasley cast spells to shield the castle. Visual effects supervisor Tim Burke calls it 'the mother of all shields'. The spells and charms that create this barrier are unique to the films.

PROTEGO MAXIMA

Protego Maxima is the strongest version of the Shield Charm. This shield also can bounce spells back on the caster.

FIANTO DURI

Used in combination with these other spells, this charm appears to strengthen them.

REPELLO INIMICUM

This Repelling Charm specifically targets opponents. *Repello* is Latin for 'I drive away' and *Inimicum* means 'the enemy'.

FALLING UNDER A SPELL

The visual effects designers wanted the protective shield around the castle to feel organic but be invisible once it was in place. 'The idea was that, when the Death Eaters launched their spells, you would be aware of its presence again when the spells exploded on the shield,' Tim Burke explains.

BREAKING THE SPELL

The deterioration of the Hogwarts shield happens in stages. First, fine cracks appear in the surface and then patches ignite. 'We were keen to make it look like it was actually burning,' Tim says, 'with the shield itself changing its state from being solid and glassy into something more material.' As the shield collapses, burning pieces of it float down to the ground.

PIERTOTUM LOCOMOTOR

Piertotum Locomotor brings inanimate objects to life. Professor McGonagall casts this charm to animate the knight statues that line the castle walls to form another line of protection for Hogwarts. The intact knights that leapt from the Great Hall's walls and marched together were digital, but the broken and battered knights in the battle's aftermath were made from fibreglass and painted to look like stone.

CHARMED OBJECTS

Spells and charms can be cast upon objects, such as parchments, bags and living facilities, to change and enhance their abilities or capacities.

The Marauder's Map

The Marauder's Map shows the location of everyone and every location on the Hogwarts grounds with few exceptions. It also was charmed by its creators – James Potter, Sirius Black, Remus Lupin, and Peter Pettigrew – to not reveal its secrets when Severus Snape tried to use it (and to insult him!).

The effect where Remus Lupin folds up the Marauder's Map at the end of *Harry Potter and the Prisoner of Azkaban* was done practically by pulling invisible threads. The only digital effects for the map are the footsteps and the rippling words when it is seen close-up.

Whoops!

Miraphora Mina and Eduardo Lima were inspired in the creation of the folded, multilayered map by the moving staircases in Hogwarts castle and 'because Hogwarts does feel like it just goes on and on,' says Miraphora. The actual architectural drawings of the Hogwarts sets were traced over to create the map, which led to a mistake – the Room of Requirement was included on the first passes until someone finally noticed it, and then it was covered over.

Itinerarium Maraudentium

Messrs.
MOONEY, WORMTAIL,
PADFOOT & PRONGS
are proud to present

HOGWARTS

The
MARAUDER'S
MAP

'I solemnly swear that I am up to no good' (open map), 'Mischief managed' (close map)

Extension Charm

An Extension Charm creates a larger interior inside a smaller exterior. Extension Charms were used on the tent the Weasleys occupied at the Quidditch World Cup and the tent Hermione, Ron and Harry lived in as they searched for the Horcruxes.

Professor Horace Slughorn owns an hourglass charmed to make the running sand hurry or slow down depending on the quality of the current conversation. Graphic artist Miraphora Mina gave the hourglass a decidedly Slytherin style, with three silver-headed snakes forming the structure that holds the green-tinted glass.

That'll Be the Books

Hermione used an Extension Charm on a small beaded bag she filled with supplies, including, of course, books created by the graphic department. 'It was a really nice opportunity to think which ones she would have taken on her trip,' says graphic artist Miraphora Mina. At one point, '[Hermione] shakes [her bag] and there is this terrible noise of stacked books falling over,' she adds. 'Sadly, you don't get to see all of them in the film.'

Molly Weasley charms her knitting needles to craft her woollen masterpieces on their own. For this, the prop department created a mechanical device that clicks the needles back and forth, which was set behind the rows of wool.

Written by Jody Revenson

BLOOMSBURY CHILDREN'S BOOKS, Bloomsbury Publishing Plc, 50 Bedford Square, London WC1B 3DP, UK

BLOOMSBURY, BLOOMSBURY CHILDREN'S BOOKS and the Diana logo are trademarks of Bloomsbury Publishing Plc

First published in the US in 2019
First published in Great Britain in 2019 by Bloomsbury Publishing Plc.

www.bloomsbury.com

A catalogue record for this book is available from the British Library

ISBN
978 1 5266 1318 9

MANUFACTURED IN CHINA

10 9 8 7 6 5 4 3 2 1

EXPECTO PATRONUM!

PRODUCED BY:

INSIGHT EDITIONS
PO Box 3088
San Rafael, CA 94912
www.insighteditions.com

Publisher: Raoul Goff
Associate Publisher: Vanessa Lopez
Creative Director: Chrissy Kwasnik
Designer: Evelyn Furuta
Editor: Greg Solano
Editorial Assistant: Jeric Llanes
Senior Production Editor: Rachel Anderson
Senior Production Manager: Greg Steffen

Insight Editions, in association with Roots of Peace, will plant two trees for each tree used in the manufacturing of this book. Roots of Peace is an internationally renowned humanitarian organisation dedicated to eradicating land mines worldwide and converting war-torn lands into productive farms and wildlife habitats. Roots of Peace will plant two million fruit and nut trees in Afghanistan and provide farmers there with the skills and support necessary for sustainable land use.

IN MEMORIAM

Sadly, some members of the Wizarding World have passed away since the finish of Harry Potter's screen story. These include actor Richard Harris, whose Dumbledore made us all feel loved and safe; Stephenie McMillan, set decorator for all eight films; and actor Alan Rickman, who brought the always intriguing Severus Snape to the screen. We raise our wands in tribute to these talented people who brought their magic to the Harry Potter films.

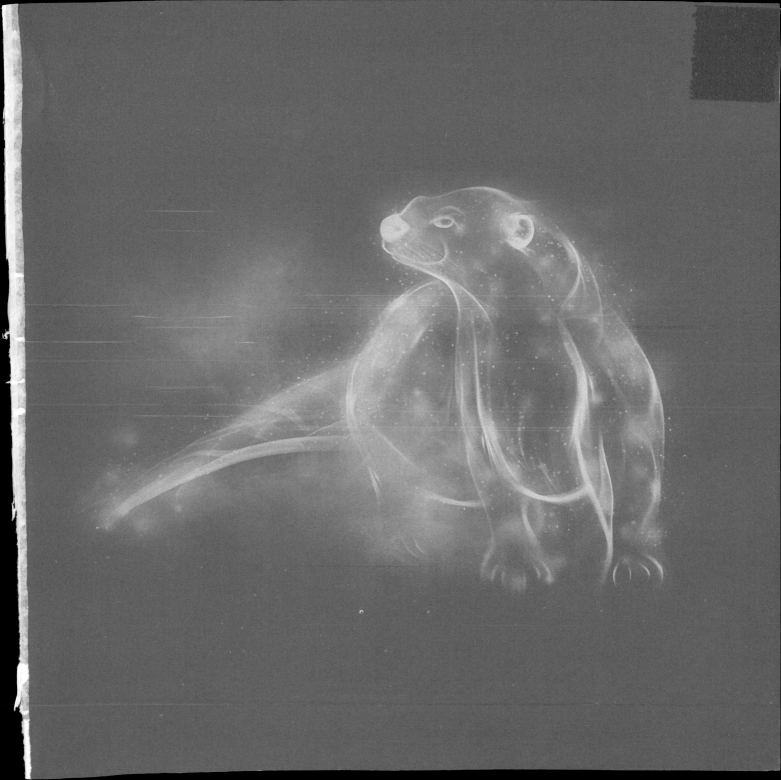

SPELLS & CHARMS